Mamabird

poems by

Katie Fesuk

Finishing Line Press
Georgetown, Kentucky

Mamabird

ACKNOWLEDGMENTS

Section i. and ii.: Quotes from Debbie Blue's *Consider the Birds* reprinted
with permission from the author.

Section iii: From ALL THE LIGHT WE CANNOT SEE by Anthony Doerr.
Copyright © 2014 by Anthony Doerr. Reprinted with the permission of
Scribner, a division of Simon & Schuster, Inc. All rights reserved.

Section v and vi: Quotes from Jonathan Franzen's "Why Birds Matter"
reprinted with permission from the author.

Publisher: Leah Maines

Editor: Christen Kincaid

Cover Art: Clay Thurston

Author Photo: Hannah Gillman of Hannah G Photography 2018

Cover Design: Elizabeth Maines McCleavy

Printed in the USA on acid-free paper.
Order online: www.finishinglinepress.com
            also available on amazon.com

Author inquiries and mail orders:
Finishing Line Press
P. O. Box 1626
Georgetown, Kentucky 40324
U. S. A.

Table of Contents

Acknowledgments

—in memory of Mary Fesuk,
the original mamabird;

for my children, Sawyer and Mary Katherine,
who made me a mamabird;

my father, Andrew "Fez" Fesuk,
who gave me lakes and oceans;

and my husband, Damian,
for wings and gills and a room of my own.

Mama

i.

The mother pelican has the greatest love of all creatures for its offspring, so the story goes, because she sacrifices herself (pierces her own breast with her beak) to feed her children with her blood... Bird observers have come to understand that there is no 'pelican in her piety.' The mother pelican doesn't peck her breast to feed her young. It's an ancient misinterpretation... We need to read and reread, imagine and reimagine. Sometimes we need to let go of what we think and go back and look again.

~from Debbie Blue, *Consider the Birds*

To Other Parents in June, Our Kids Like Kites or Birds Near the Sea

I know you, solitary gulls.

The same unseen line,
thin string, bridles us
to billowing fabric,
our children
harnessing salt wind.
That's far enough.
The ocean is vast, and you,
so fledgling, so peep,
so babybird.

We wave long arms
watching that undertow.
In similar avian hymns,
it's deep out there.
Have a rest.

Teetering to foamy edges,
we rub sunscreen on their wingbones.

We mamabird:
drink some water,
eat a cracker,
don't throw sand.

Our tented choral chant
travels small but parallel distances,
tidal arias:
please don't swim where
I can't reach you,
too far into that blue
blue world.

We step into this wet, shelled margin,
wave-shaped shore.
In voices grounding, diurnal,

we are a flock of tricolored umbrellas,
calling our children.

My Children, Their Light

My boy and girl covered in suds,
their bodies lean and slender bands
of muscle and laughter,
skin glowing with summer's light.
Perched on the tub's edge,
I hold white towels.

It's not hard to imagine
that the smooth, rising ridges
of their scapulae
might be wings—

wings that could unfold,
dew-shining bone
and feather leaving sunlit drops
hanging in the air
before they fly
someplace new.

Self-Made

Across the crimson bricks
of Faneuil Hall where artists entertain
daily masses, I watch as my daughter Mary
moves away from me,
from her father and brother,
summoned by music that compels her to dance.
The drummer sits low on an upside-down paint can,
smiling. His refrain sounds like an island I'd like to see.
She is four, filled toe to tip with song
as though bells chime for her all day.
And they do, and I do—high note of my own heart,
deepest chord without name,
the wonder
that she is at once mine
and so wildly not mine.
Drumbeats fill her belly. She shakes, a natural.
Her hands twinkle. The crowd nods
at her freedom, a kind most of us
have misplaced.
Raucous percussion of homespun rhythm
booms from metal sinks and pots,
spatula drumsticks, tin cans, pantry items
balanced on cooling racks for resonance.
Mary Katherine's feet flap, small wings.
She shares his ecstasy in the commonplace:
music from wayward spoons and lost strainers,
his self-made symphony
and what she makes of the air with her tiny body.
I sense whole years like this—
her hands and feet
and shock of blonde hair, her belonging.
Her separateness.
I do not know from what strange kitchen
my daughter has collected this bravery,
but I pray that she will not, cannot, stop swaying.

Onomastics for My Kids, or, How Naming Can Be Like Earth Science

You're better off asking:
why is it warm at the equator
and cold at the poles?
How does rain form?

These questions are old, hard to explain.
My children are learning the weight
of their names, how to carry
the words we have given them—
to write and know each letter.

Things move from atmosphere
to lithosphere
in a process that determines
the character of an environment.

When their names are fired
to signal trouble, loosed from lips
as a blown kiss, they learn
what it feels like to be
summoned across a room,
down a long staircase.

Names like a wave, spoken for their own sake,
remind me that that my son's hands
have grown big,
clipped nails like crescent moons
falling from his body.

My daughter at midnight, arms thrown
around a stuffed caterpillar,
brings all the world into her orbit.

But like veins occupying a rock fissure,
its fault, the sadness of names begins.
So early for both of my children to look
at me through tears, demand

how dare you?

My son in kindergarten, bewildered,
says the boys in class laugh,
call his last name *funny*, his middle name *girly*.
He's confused by his parents'
insistence to call him anything else
but wind and rainfall and seawater.
Coal beds, river deltas, salt marshes.

My daughter in preschool struggles with grips
and pencils, keeping straight lines.
She wants to know
why her double name is so long,
cries when learning to maneuver
its curves. *Why so many letters?*
I'm tired. We take small steps.
Initials first, one word,
one word plus one letter.
In spring, the whole thing must be written.
Why not nautilus, volcanos, bright coral?

Ask instead: how does air temperature
help desert formation?
Do topography and ocean currents
influence the weather?

The answers are what they are,
driven by sunlight,
same as those names:
carbon cycling through oceans,
shells, erosion, rocks, birth.
Upwellings of deep water.
Whole hunks of white cliff.

My sea, my trees:
they washed up on my shore.

Dear Stars

From his second grade teacher,
my nephew learns about hieroglyphs,
scrawls from another country and era.
He likes the ones with wings.
"A is a bird," he says.
"Lots of hieroglyphs are birds."
Neither time nor place
can change our desire
to see words take flight,
feathered utterances
in a blue expanse of sky,
language turned to ibis and gull.
When he speaks of canabic jars,
I imagine women writing with kohl
on their own faces.
"C is a cup tilted sideways
with tea pouring out."
Yes, the pouring in, holding heat,
letting go.
He draws a tomb and pyramids,
remembers more: M is an owl.
Cryptic, stormy predator
my mother keeps writing
from spirit world to my own,
hooting in its tree off Hadaway Road.
M for Mary, cosmic love letter
from my daughter's namesake
flying past the Japanese maple
we planted after she died.
Dear stars, forgive me how much
I comb my child's long hair,
the color of each good sunset,
its silk in my grip,
her every sound a dove
cupped in hand,
carved into the mountains around us,
bird heartbeat in my palms.
Feathers everywhere I go.

Two Kinds of Blue

When we look
at the spiral galaxy closest to our own,
we see it as it was
two million years ago.
My children remember being small
and tossing plaid blankets in the backyard,
searching for clover and red ants
in the Georgia grass,
returning to me
with yellow and white flowers.
They placed each one, dappled
tints of our yard, in my hair.

When it rains
and we drive by a rainbow,
Mary Katherine says *Light
has all the colors, Mommy.
Two kinds of blue, purple, red, green, orange...*
Do I tell her
that if the Earth were swallowed
by a black hole,
we may not even notice?

She made a color spectrum at school,
so we spun the circle on a stick,
mottling all the world's
possible shades. Sometimes,
we are living
in an alternate universe of dark matter.

Paul McCartney didn't know if *Yesterday*
was someone else's song when he thought of it.
Hard to know which story
began with another.
I'm not sure if my children are my own
or if we are holograms of light.
Between wakefulness and sleep,

I see their faces, spinning
towards twilight, kaleidoscopic.

Windswept

After the babies were born,
my thighs and breasts
looked like windswept deserts
of Africa and Asia, aerial photos
taken after a sandstorm
rearranged grains
into slinking lines
visible from a helicopter,
evidence the wind had worked
its signature into the ground.
My body was proof
that the tiny forms I rocked
to sleep had been inside me once,
breathed strange gills
and beat rapid hearts,
blinked veiled lids.
My middle swelled
like a ship's boards on its maiden
voyage—taking in all the water
it could without bursting, trying
joists' and posts' integrity.
My body did as all bodies do:
its best. Some parts assumed
their earlier shape, others
couldn't recover that old topography.
And who could blame them after so much reaching?
Newer skin appeared
like violet lightning.
I dimmed bedroom lights,
cringed when my soapy
hand touched the raised paint brush
strokes in morning showers.
What remains are lines
like fading plums, rose skies at night,
scars that stretch to show
where I was rounder
than a pomegranate,
full as a magnolia's crown.

Grief, Stitched with Flowers

Of the magician she saw yesterday,
my six-year-old niece tells me
He took a ball from his pocket,
put it in his mouth,
and pulled out
a scarf stitched with flowers!

Magic, shapeshifting, hope's physics.
Don't we always want
that direst thing lifted up in the desperate
but quiet moment before sleep?
That stars trailing
their colossal dust and heat
will stop and share
that fire, make their energy and blaze
take shape right next to us?

Here it is… your mother's heart
good again, your son's bruise
gone, that ragged scar erased,
loneliness unpacked, pain unfelt,
a knot of grief ironed flat and blown
away. In its place an emerald
or sapphire, handful
of petals, twelve seconds
of comfort, old pennies and jacks,
your zen like a pocket square,
rain where there was
none, your name in the sand or mud.

A ball into a scarf, she says again.
In his mouth!
Eat one thing. It becomes
something else. But I shouldn't bother
her about transubstantiation,
about what happens when, in the midst
of prayer and in the path of all those falling

stars, one eats dread and finds
it has turned, like hard candy, to relief.
Sometimes, I will tell her one day,
it is not a sleight of hand, love.
Not just charm.

As a man's mouth converts
toy to kerchief,
the earth can change
the arrangement of atoms
and molecules, shift
even a solid ruby ball
to soft cloth, covered
in green stems and violets.

Poem Written on the Occasion of My Daughter's Chalk Drawing, in Which I Look Like a Jellyfish

She tells a story in proportions:
my frame, weird medusa, propels
through water like a banshee
through white birch.
Hair a seagrass pile
in a mangrove swamp.

She says *You have curly legs,*
tracing gangly lost tentacles
that carry my fishbowl face,
my electric eel smile.
No eyes. My nose an abalone.
I am octopus.
I am oceanic winter tree
with a left ear small as plankton.
My right, ten times its size,
is a deep concentric shell.
I hear her in color:
bioluminescent blues and yellows.

Let her always see
me this way: Cassiopeia,
upside-down jellyfish.
My arms one shoreline,
entire body one oyster,
wishful in its ratio
beneath a seaweed orb head
as I carry her, my ephyra,
across the ocean's open surface.

The Naughty Spoon

My mother chased
me with a spatula
from kitchen to living room
to front door, threatening
to tickle to my feet,
break the spoon on my behind.
Near family photos, my father hangs
a paddle that cracked
on his ass during college hazing.
So picture me at six years old,
belly-down on a dock,
leaning into Lake Winnipesaukee
to grab a dingy brush
on incoming waves. Me,
who'd been warned explicitly
Do not go near the water.
Then belly-down again
across my father's lap,
staring through a mustard hallway
at my mother,
who'd told him to spank me.
My friends now draw
unhappy faces
in black marker on backs
of wooden spoons,
keep them in purses
when their children act up.
When they growl,
Do you want
the naughty spoon?
I sweat, silenced, and see
the dock, a hairbrush washing in
from open water,
its bristled and wooden dare.

A Thousand Names and More

"...and whatsoever Adam called every living creature, that was the name thereof. And Adam gave names to all cattle, and to the fowl of the air, and to every beast of the field..." Genesis 2:19

Even last week's orange moon, a sphere that set so big
and close to the ground that it looked
like trees had birthed round fire into the sky, had no name.
What will we call this season in me?
I save words on yellow notes inside desk drawers,
whisper them in prayers on the drive home,
lay them on the table like blueprints before your father each night.
In another world, I could give you a thousand names and more:
birch, elm, chinaberry, bark. I'd name you indigo.
I'd name you linen and silk and November.
You would be book, sonnet, syllable, revelation.
You would be psalm. You, heartbeat, sacrament, silver, iris.
You, mango and stone fruit and soil and amber.
I'd call you the smell of burning leaves,
cicadas that sent me to sleep when you
were barely the size of a peppercorn.
You could be named the ocean's warmth against my ankles
the day I suspected you within my body,
or the word—if there is one—for my face after that
as I watched other people's children swim around me,
considered what color your hair would be, how bright your eyes,
whether your voice would even out to song someday.
I'd name you pear and darling and babushka.
You would be called moonlight.
I'd name you the way it feels when you move
within my belly, balanced at the highest lip
of a rollercoaster before it barrels to the ground.
I would call you that dip, that fall. That fear.
You roll in me like a great fish, a speckled whale, but also the ocean.
You, the dancer's feet, but also flamenco, also notes rising.
I'd name you the last drop of wine in a glass by the fireplace,
the grape it came from, and better,
its vineyard swallowing up hillsides in promise.

You should be called the quiet force
that stills me when I watch your father move across a room,
my silent wish for a way to explain devotion,
as if words or names are ever enough.
Your name should be the same as white columns
on his childhood home. I'd name you the lake from mine.
Bone of my bone, my child, my son,
I can only give you the word that others will say,
the one somebody will love when you become a man.
You are the poem my body writes on the earth.

Bird

ii.

Mercy not sacrifice. Imagine the beauty of the scene—some wild flourishing of life, instead of death for life. Scapegoats would not have to take the blame for the fact that none of us lives up to our ideals. Those accused of witch craft could come down off the stake—teach Aristotle about medicinal herbs. The gawky and awkward, loose and unattached would not be shunned. There would be shiploads of children and soldiers and indigenous peoples, the maimed, the ostracized, the fat, the sad alive and well among us. The dodo bird, the sea cow, the blue-footed booby, the pelican free of oil—grace in flight.

~from Debbie Blue, *Consider the Birds*

What to Call Me When I Grow Up

Start with names I've never considered before.
Not like when I insisted on being called
by my middle name, Marie.
Not that name the Ouija board
spelled in stuttered arcs,
balanced between young knees
in wavering candlelight from my bathroom.

Not Christine from Dallas,
the character I pretended for my parents
on slow Fridays when I thought
they couldn't see me through cowgirl hat
and drawl. Not names I wrote in the sand
with my toes when boys
trailed close behind me and Sarah, both
newly menstruating, running beside
a pod of dolphins shallow-leaping
in Jekyll Island's surf.

Playing night tag on the resort lawn,
we heard what I had only heard
about from boys on the bus in fourth grade:
the humid buzz of newlyweds
coming from a second-story sliding door,
careless, open wide.
As we giggled, shushed one another,
we didn't move, fearful
we'd be discovered in our discovering.

I want to be called *that* something breathy,
what you call a woman who then stepped
out to the porch for a cigarette.
She wore no more than a thin white shift
and stretched her cat-like body
towards the moon.
We bolted like criminals.

Name me that primal thing
that blew through her dark hair
into the piña colada haze she'd left behind
where, before we ran, a male voice
gave its deep-hearted *amen*.
In the starlight,
I'm sure she nodded.
Winked right at us,
stood like lambs in a pasture.

Carol Burnett, Inebriated

Little did we know when I was seven
that it was probably not Annie's orphan
dresses that mesmerized me. Miss Hannigan
tumbled comfortably backwards into an ivory
pedestal tub full of freshly brewed gin, made
a pass at Daddy Warbucks, bald head and all.
I was hooked.

What must that gin have tasted like
as she ladled another helping into
a slim goblet made for aperitif and juleps,
as she lapped the drip-drops that fell from her nose
and forehead, as she strained her string of pearls free
of the devil's juice? Witch hazel and relief,
tonic and grain? Oh, it must have been wonderful.

Could women be so flippant with a wink,
a sway of dangerous hip flexor, a brush
of bare shoulder against suit jacket? A flip
of the wrist that sent cigarette ashes circling
and drifting to the ground where children
without mothers would step with bare feet?
Her carelessness intoxicated; she was awful.

It was Grace in the end with her proper curls
and mellifluous voice who won Daddy Warbucks,
as it should be. Grace always wins.
When I watched each evening after dinner, I must have
secretly coveted bathtub gin, smoke rings, record players,
the obvious heat between Rooster and Lily dancing.

Soon, on an Island

When the sliver moon
is a hook
from which we hang
a drowsy day, my silk nightslip,
and painted maracas from the village,

there will be palm fronds
to wave slowly, lemon rind
to spoon on tongues, sand
between our toes,
sea water in navels.

When you say with your hands,
I am the ocean come to give you
this coral, this shell, this storm
and my body tells you,
I am the island bathed
in starfish, lava rock, Spanish moss,
casita doors will open
to salt air and coconut.

Soon, love, we will eat sugar
from mouths of rum
glasses, rocking like
tide and shore
behind the mosquito net.

We'll dream the trees
have learned to speak:
ikal, mariposa, llueve,
they will say, wooden vowels
rattling those moon-hung gourds
to a rhumba.

Anniversary, Milky Way

The first time I saw an actual galaxy,
you showed me
I had to lay down, look up.
Sand in my hair, boardwalk on my back,
feet dusted with Carolina sand.
Tides returned their guttural swoosh.
No other glow seeped in from cities,
only the moon's face on the Atlantic.

Our galaxy, that Milky Way,
its clarity of untold faint stars,
wisped along coal-black cover
and vanishing celestial bodies
long burned out—a band
of light to wrap around one's finger,
a heaven I missed,
too close to see until night.
Astronomic ghosts
strewn like dandelion fluff
from a child's hand,
draped like sash
over Venus' hips.

Oceans and tides. Zenith, equinox,
canyons. Unnamed moons and nebulas,
we can be like that:
center of our own solar system
that cannot be stared at directly.
Part of a whole galaxy
made real, our food the many stars,
our children new planets, bodies
spun into being
after a meteor collides.

Hide and Seek

Been chasing the muses around my home for days.
They got the idea of hide and seek from watching my children
while I huddle in the closet, take bubble baths,
crouch near spider-webbed garage shelves
counting *3, 2, 1… Ready or not?*
My pencils are sharpened, pens uncapped.

They hunker down in baskets, silent
under the stairs, slipping into white cabinets.
Can't find them in the *Star Wars* puzzles
or rock collection, cicada skins
peeled from our dogwoods.
Not in the laundry room or crumpled corners
of fitted sheets.

They are not in our pet graveyard—two hamsters,
three African frogs, a crawfish named Cilantro,
four hermit crabs, and two good dogs.
They're waiting for more drama, something
cosmopolitan. All I can offer is the Australian Shepard
pulling meat wrappers out of the trash,
a Japanese Maple dropping blood-red leaves.

Would that giant oak in Maggie Valley bring them out to play?
Half the tree in Cold Mountain's growing shadow,
the other bathed in fading sunshine, a mirror,
its trunk a barky meridian between one world and the next.
Divine proportion of crown above, roots below,
curious looking-glass, half the leaves grim ash,
the rest set ablaze. A dark-pretty veil.

But Calliope shrouds herself upstairs,
throws the comforter over her body.
The others duck under the sofa, scattering
dust-bunnies, strum my husband's guitar
in the basement. They stir up fireplace cinders
with their toes and light one strike-anywhere

match after another.

If they would only show themselves,
braid my hair and paint my fingernails
like ancient fish scales.
It is a game. I'm IT,
looking for these other daughters
in a home filled with blank reams of paper,
blurring charcoal in chiaroscuro,
drawing, again and again, the same oak.

Mama

iii.

And is it so hard to believe that souls traveled those paths… might harry the sky in flocks, like egrets, like terns, like starlings? That great shuttles of souls might fly about, faded but audible if you listen closely enough? They flow above the chimneys, ride the sidewalks, slip through your jacket and shirt and breastbone and lungs, and pass out through the other side, the air a library and the record of every life lived, every sentence spoken, every word transmitted still reverberating within it.

~from Anthony Doerr, *All the Light We Cannot See*

My Mom and Stevie Wonder

Stevie Wonder touched
my mother's hand
at a ramshackle smoky bar
on the water near Boston.
From her tone, the curled
grin, the way she rubs
her hands together lost in memory—
I like to think that he did more
than touch it.
Spare matches filled her apron.
He sat at her table before going onstage,
wearing that wide bright smile.
She was young and beautiful, Cleopatra
darts from black liquid liner
framing her eyes.
Maybe Stevie's piano hand
closed gently over hers, feeling
her electric pulse, and he said
Mary, oh Mary, what a girl!
How about a whiskey?
Perhaps even a pat on the ass
before she spun her cocktail tray
toward the bartender.
When she returned,
heels and ice cubes clicking,
maybe he caressed the wrist
a second time. Maybe he touched her
soft cheek, the skin that would captivate
my father, pulled her to his lap.
And just maybe my mother leaned in
to his whispers, took a sip of Stevie's drink
before tapping him on the nose,
and giggled *no thanks,*
swinging her hips
to the next two-top.

Moonshine

I imagined tiny men
polishing a crescent in the night sky
with soft small blankets—
dusting away particles,
dark matter, astral powder.
Drunk off its light, in revelry.

My mother always kept
a bottle of moonshine in our freezer
near aluminum foil stacks of cash,
which she stuffed like fish
or bread into Ziploc bags.
I vaguely understood
its potency but loved its name.

She barely drank, an easy blusher,
but sometimes, whether to impress
or to terrify,
she would take the clear bottle,
loosening its silver screw top
like a Christmas star
then say, *Watch this.*

On My Parents' Thirtieth Anniversary, Before I Really Understood Irony and Beauty

for my mom, who was scared of bees

My mother missed Georgia,
dreaded the return to New England's winters.
When Southern women began wearing
golden frogs, toads, and snakes as pins,
bedazzled with emeralds and rubies,
my father presented two bumblebee pins
in a velvet blue pouch like bugs in the belly
of a tiny kangaroo. She held the gilded pieces
in her palm, a peculiar communion.
On her lapel and nearest to her heart
she pinned the bees.
For the rest of dinner,
her hands crept back to that lapel,
fingering the wings, feeling the sapphire eyes
and precious thorax. Pleased.
We finished our meal less than a mile
from Sturbridge Village
where she once worked in a white bonnet
and sometimes, in the act, chopped heads
off of chickens.
I could never picture that sight.
My mother. The ax.
Her dark hair coming loose in the cap.
The bird's nerves that caused
movement after death.
But that night I started to see it,
the distance between one time or place
and the next, the chopping block
and my mother's hands and apron.
And she didn't flinch.
Not once.

Healing

When she was twenty, my mother crammed
pennies into her hospital robe
pockets so doctors would let her go
outside. She received last rites
twice. The weight of boiling water
her mother threw still singed
her shoulders. Her father's reassuring
smell—Juicy Fruit and cigars—gone
as the flesh from her frame. When
the wound in her gut refused
to heal, a family nun on rounds plucked
the crude wooden cross
from her own rosary belt, planted
it in bandaged gauze, decreed
Hail Mary's and Glory Be's. She left
that room with her flock
of holy women.
Left my mother Mary with startling
blue eyes and the face of a Madonna,
my Mary, my mother, to whom I
was a vague hope,
under that weight.
Mom healed overnight.
By morning, only a seam remained.

Kitchen Table

*"Does then the cosmic space we dissolve in taste of us? Do the angels reclaim
only what is theirs, their own outstreamed existence, or sometimes, by
accident, does a bit of us get mixed in?" ~Rilke*

Where it might be now is anyone's guess.

I held onto anything
belonging to her for years: Anye wallets,
hair scarves, Aunt Linda's costume jewelry,
bud vases, embroidered dish towels, bonds
bearing her signature, the ones
I couldn't cash because once,
she inked those old blue slips.
I held and held and held.

So imagine: a whole table.

Trestle, pedestal, post.
Six chairs, a leaf.
Home to candles and sticky notes
and Nana's Irish linens.
Hours of algebra and essays—
baklava in thin crisp layers,
penmanship dents in all
right and remembered spots.

Between dovetail and joist,
in rings left by cups of vanilla coffee,
if she remains part angel wing,
part stardust and lemon square,
I could get her back, pull
a dining chair up to that old table,
whisk some butter into sunshine
with lemon rind and cinnamon
in mixing bowls, call that
unseen muse back to the meal.

Bless My Mother's Nightgowns

Bless my mother's nightgowns,
the ones I've started sleeping in,
the ones I took from her closet, after.
Pink with lace collar,
turquoise caftan with black stitching,
deep peony robe with pockets
that still held tissues.
Bless me in these nightgowns in my bed
after the children are asleep
and I've hid this grief from my husband another day.
Bless the other things I took
from her bedside table, greedy daughter
hoarding her mother's keepsakes
like a small animal: several journals,
old driver's license, relic filled with saint bones,
butterfly earrings,
wallet-size pamphlet of John Donne poems.
Bless these robes that make me feel like a child
sleeping next to her shallow night breaths,
the same kind she took in those last hours,
my body draped over hers,
reading her poems.
Bless the holiday cookie cutters
and set of dishes etched in gardenias.
Bless her perfume,
teacups, empty
notebooks and prayer
books. Bless the hollow
space inside me
too big to mention—black
hole, supernova of absence,
implosion.
Bless the old blue coat
that seems to hold
her smell no matter how
many times it's worn.

Sometimes When I Open My Mouth to Speak, I Hear My Mother's Voice

While the rest of my home
is washed in winter darkness,
our Christmas tree is still up
in the living room, its many-beaded
string of lights an odd rosary
weaving through the dying arms
of evergreen. I don't want
to take it down—the tree speaks
to something like a bird
that spreads its wings in my throat,
a holy dove flying.
Sometimes, when I open my mouth,
I hear my mother's voice instead.

It reminds me of the magi,
one star calling out
to wise men for their attention,
how wisdom meant heeding what was written
in the sky, that winter is not the only time
to follow one's star
in whatever desert heaven
it may appear.

My mother's voice,
her voice in mine
making the invisible visible.
In that evergreen, there could be
whole constellations:
Pleiades, Andromodae, Ursa Major—
their many stars formed together,
traveling at similar velocities
then dissolving
into smaller circles
of moving light.

Let Down, Kennestone Hospital

Ever been in Target or Kroger,
and a breastfeeding child
is back at home?
You hear someone else's baby
wailing in the produce aisle.
You're holding the diapers
you came here for,
so your new mother's breasts
ache like a dammed river,
then release their milk.
So much for the hour alone,
the clean shirt.

After we took my mother
off breathing machines,
let her own blood and heart
do as they pleased,
doctors said she'd pass
in five to ten minutes.
For days, she'd listened to me
reading poetry books,
stepping into bathrooms every hour
to relieve my breasts that filled
with useless milk.

Twelve hours later,
Mom's eyes were Sphinx-like,
crescent lakes of white, blue iris.
Her chest rose and fell.
She waited for us to leave.

At home, I held my little Mary,
sleeping with eyes half-open,
same white lakes and blue iris
as her namesake.

I'd never feed her from my body again.

Has a Palpable Form of Grief Overtaken My Life?

*~Self-inquiry for Homeopathic Tinctures to Use
When Addressing Emotional Component of an Illness*

Do you mean, like an egg?
As in the way a chicken
unties one from its body
to be eaten
by the world?

A piece of glass
that could contain
a beautiful thing,
but has been broken already,
reflects only a shrinking body?

Or by palpable, do
you mean when, having dreamed
of my mother,
I'm upright in bed, half-smiling, still
sleepy, before I realize her touch
on my face was imagination?

I cannot have back
the long wharf walk
over the Charles River Bridge
to the science museum when
bone spurs on her feet
made her wince.

To feel her voice
in the Filene's changing room,
its communal undressing, women
with their saggy breasts
and bodies I didn't yet
understand (*It's okay, we all
have the same parts*),
I'd take those spurs

on my own heels and toes.

The cold burn of Ben and Jerry's
off Beacon Street stung
and delighted me,
like lightning bolts
from the museum generator,
its magnetism that drew
like forces to like forces.

Seven years. Her absence
is a wild strike,
her name in the sky
an icy electric charge,
her pain, my bones.

What to Pack, What to Keep

She hadn't worn one in twenty years.
Not since our yellow New Hampshire cottage
with lucid lake water
where we spied olive walleye,
plump shadows of grass carp beneath our boat.

Bring the blue bathing suit
in the second drawer, she murmured,
trip to Winnie this weekend.
Her body folded between two hospital bed rails,
my mother spoke of her old dresser
waiting to be decanted to nothing
but lace.

Twenty-one grams or otherwise,
she knew the weight of her soul
that evening in the emergency room.
It traveled, her brokenness a lumen
weaving this *now* with one *then*:
some Friday two decades past
when she packed a swimsuit.

Maybe she's grown buoyant like that,
telling me, my father, my children in dreams
to watch Saunders Bay for fireworks.
She's gossamer and rosy-cheeked
in puddles of light, wading knee-high
through glinting lake water
in her royal blue suit.

Denise, My Mother Is Not in This Teacup, So I'll Take the Monkey

after Denise Duhamel's "Expired"
for Mary and Andrew "Fez" Fesuk

If someone laid out
    all my mother's things
and said, *take something of hers*
    to remember her by,

that poor someone would tire
    of my indecision, my arboresque hush.
Fixed as a magnolia, a myrtle, a sweetgum,
    I'd halt, wonder how to unzip

myself from throat to pelvis,
    slide a pull-tab to uncouple teeth
and unchain my chest like a winter coat.
    I'd place my heart, lungs, all viscera

on a table, glistening and heavy. *Let me*
    see, she's in here somewhere.
A macabre secondhand operation. It's what
    I must have looked like

to the couple who handled the estate sale.
    Mom's 1979 Colony Park wagon
had a bumper sticker: "I Brake for Antiques,"
    and these men dug through three stories

of bygones, *all* of them stretched out
    cadavers, end to end, on bunks. Each toe
circled with string and tagged a dollar or five.
    One room for Nana's dolls and clothes, another

for Skip's Yankees cards, my dad's olive green army men,
    a child's microscope set, snow sleds, cigar-making tools,
cast iron skillets, enough teapots and salt cellars to line
    a path straight down Highway 41

to Yester-Year Antiques and Flea Market where, on Saturdays mornings,
       Mom and I grabbed Mary Kay lip gloss, mismatched
silver, flapper hats, and prayer cards featuring
       the Virgin Mary and Saint Jude to reclaim our lost

things. We bought popcorn and sodas near the organ grinder
       with a red-vested monkey on a leash.
The monkey danced, collected tips in her crimson kilim fez.
       She'd leap to my shoulder, upturned hat and tassel

begging for coins, so exotic and out of place
       in Georgia among clapping shoppers, I didn't know
at twelve to be sad for her. I didn't know to be sad.
       Forgive me, Denise, it took years to learn:

my mother is not in this or any teacup. Not
       in scarab bracelets, recipe books, or Montblanc pens
I've hoarded, not sewing cushions swiped when shoppers weren't looking
       from gurneys of *for sale* trinkets.

If you could lay out our things one more time,
       I'll rescue that capuchin from Yester-Year,
    wear her ruby fez like a sage,
       let her ride shotgun in the station wagon,

throw pennies out the window
       at kudzu and Shirley poppies, twirl her busted leash
to jump rope at pit stops, clank our cymbals in my mother's name.
       We'll talk shit about that crusty organ grinder

from Hiram and blast Barry Manilow tapes
       and break all the antiques, head for Morocco
or Egypt where I can seal myself, box-pin to top-stop,
       together again, an empty vessel.

Bird

iv.

All these birds, insects, animals, reptiles, whistling, whispering, screaming, howling, croaking, fish in their kinds teeming, plants thrusting and struggling, life in its million, its billion forms, the greatest concentration of living things on this continent...

~from Marjory Stoneman Douglas, *Florida: The Long Frontier*

Guidelines for Submission

Candling: a step in the egg grading process that lets the egg grader look inside the egg without breaking it to judge its quality

First, you should crack a raw egg
        on your head, let its lost
                potential and washed bloom seep down

                    over your meringue hair and shell shoulders.

You should shudder and feel dirty, too,
        awaiting a *bain marie* that will not come.

Preferably this happens in front of a candling audience
        so that someone is there

                to witness the awkward paleness
                of your skin.

You should be tempered and wearing thin

        cotton undergarments, light or pastel islet
                so there is more of you to weep and glow

                with humiliation
                    if a breaker in the audience

        should hold some candlelight close against your back,

lighting through transparent flesh
        to expose the blood inside.

        You, swathed in albumen, will flutter like a chalaza,
            covered in egg, well-beaten,
                lit up from behind.

        You'll cradle
            a heart that can't help but beat,

mouthing at last,

what is it you want me to do?

When the House and Night Hum

The ear wants that noise
to be hummingbird or heron
wing, iceberg letting go
its layers, slow ache of whirling
fan and clothes dryer.
Wants it to be neighbors'
children, a lover's
throaty awakening, cherries falling
on the ground, something
even one hundred miles away
that only you can hear.
Instead, it's all the things
you forgot
to do today and may never
do, shattering,
quiet and slow,
in your dumb face.

Mise En Place

"Could this be madness, this?" ~Sylvia Plath

Beyond all dusky upstairs rooms,
their doors fastened tight, locked by skeleton
keys I've lost in some drawer
of the mind, yeast feeds.
This dough I mixed without knowing.
This hidden swelling leaven.
Did I knead, shape, and proof
in witchy haste? Flee
down halls past other ingresses,
descend a dozen rectangles of ancient wood,
fling salt in my wake
past entrances sealed by tarnished knobs?
Even in that closeted darkness,
an oven, and somehow: heat.
A bitter meal bakes in shadow.
I step outside, close the front
handle on the whole house.

That sad rich bread
stays warm in its wardrobe.
Sours. Keeps rising.
Tucked in a round wicker basket,
covered in light blue dishcloth,
left inside a dark cupboard,
such bread will not cool.
From the porch, I drift towards bare oak trees,
yard littered with pine boughs from a winter storm,
black street where everyone I know
drives past on their way somewhere.

On a Scale of One to Ten, What Is Your Pain Level?

It's infinity
or less than zero.

It's seven
if that means you'll give me enough morphine

to make this sensation of swooning
and stuck knives subside.

It's everything broken
where the light tries to get in.

It's all the cells
my body doesn't recognize as home.

On a scale of one to ten, what I want you
to understand

one hundred percent is this:
I turn inside out enough

to unearth one painless truth, like a shining giant
wave of electromagnetic energy

to project the story of my bones,
singing what's in my blood.

What's Buried There

She was the first dog
to make our son cackle.
That dog who dug ridiculous tunnels
through Georgia red clay
under fences, cost us
apartments and midnight trips
to emergency vets.

Small terrier with a piercing bark
who pissed on everything
in our first house—
who nearly gave her life
bringing two pups into the world,
the third one stillborn.

Dog I swore I hated
but cradled when her coat
swelled to welts
after bee-stings,
and again in a blanket
when some December,
she dug one of those holes
to the neighbor's yard and tumbled,
clumsy girl, straight
into a pond of dizzying goldfish.

Dog that could make my husband
cry, dog whose cool body
I discovered in the basement,
alone at the end
of a work day when I had to call
back, tell him it was a seizure.

Dog who knew that life brewed
in my belly and laid on top of it
for months to feel our babies
kick and roll—first one,

then the other.

My five-year-old asks whether
his dog, the little one
whose stubby tail he recollects in dreams,
crawled to heaven—*where Nana is.*

We buried her near the apple tree
in a space that remains unmarked
but which the earth will turn
to kudzu or wildflower,
will mark what's buried there.

Wayward

What if my words
came back to me,
those lost lambs?
If—from the four corners
of the earth
where they have been hiding
with their thick coats
and strong necks
and deep and lovely bleating
over long distances—

they came back strong
as winds and rainstorms and shocks
of lightning?
If they let me hold them,
let me speak
with their tongues
and be a lamb, too,
the lamb *and* the shepherd
and the staff?

I wish they were
safe in my own pastures
where nothing
should be lost.
Would I be whole then,
spoken, a new body if
they came home
to graze and assemble
and be fed?

Tinnitus and the Say-So

Like emergency vehicles hum
the high pitch of the universe
wheeling freely. Like a dial turned
all the way right, a frequency for whales
and submarines, the deep's whistle.
Like sudden cotton
between ossicle and drum
or cupped invisible hand over
ear lobe and pinna.
Silence before the inner siren.
I freeze, as though ready to receive
a radio message, shrill static.

When I go to where
the bell calls, raptured
by comet, transmogrified
into light waves, (and what if
they aren't waves
at all, but circles?)
someone watching might
recall: *it was as if she heard*
a say-so, four fingers
over her ear canal, thumb to chin
like holding a tiny speaker,
closed her eyes,
opened them dizzy wide,
then poof!

Mama

v.

One reason that wild birds matter—ought to matter—is that they are our last, best connection to a natural world that is otherwise receding... The house finch outside your window is a tiny and beautifully adapted living dinosaur... After Shakespeare's King Lear steps down from the throne, he pleads with his two elder daughters to grant him some vestige of his former majesty. When the daughters reply that they don't see a need for it, the old king bursts out: 'O, reason not the need!' To consign birds to oblivion is to forget what we're the children of.

~from Jonathan Franzen, "Why Birds Matter"

Sometimes I Like to Be Lost

Once, before I was born, my father
came home from a yard sale with a fiddle.
He intended to teach himself.
Another night, stepping onto a porch
after a meal and stiff drink,
he and his friends were astounded
to look up and find more stars than sky.

He can't remember
what we talked about on the phone last night.
Or the night and nights before.
I resent my phone anyhow—
all the reaching, the expectation of availability,
the explanation of my whereabouts.
Sometimes, I like to be lost.

He missed dinners last spring
and masks surprise in his voice when he calls
only to find us out of town with the children.
Conversations—their high points like dollops
of color on a canvas—circle. Repeat. Develop patterns.
In his mind, something blooms. Dulls.

On Thanksgiving, settled
into an armchair near the fire, drink in hand,
he can tell me what it felt like at nine years old
to stand on a winter curb shouting numbers and nickels
into the cold with a twine-tied pile
of *Worcester Gazettes* at his feet, his breath
a fog. Later, the coins' metal sang in his sewn trouser pocket
as he biked home to eat buttered toast.

The best job he ever had was selling pots and pans
door-to-door in college. The spoils he earned
from peddling cookware made him feel flush,
free enough that he and Paul and Francis cut out on hot days,
swam in the Reservoir, drank cold beers.

He knows how much of each 1964 paycheck
was left after taxes, after paying bills, gas for the car.
He can tell you the make, model, paint color,
and engine hum of every automobile he ever bought.
He can tell you about the metal plate in his head,
the one in his knee,
the number and taste of rainbow trout
he caught in 1967 versus 1976
and how many times

he drove between Barre and Bangor
selling butterfly valves.

Days he lived in Chicago,
high dives off long white boards,
times he heard the Rolling Stones
on the Chevy's radio as he drove down Pleasant Street.
How many onions his father could eat,
raw and peeled like an apple
with a can of sardines and a beer.

Number of steps from the rented room's back door
to the Hull rocks bathed in Atlantic foam
during that first winter with Mary.
The landlord's spanakopita and baklava. 1969.
2009. He's forgotten her last words,
but he knows all the grave markers
at St. John's—which elm, which hill,
which stone pieta leads the way.

These are numbers and days he can find
easily as an archer's target,
a pheasant's lifting wing.
Clear as the line between bent rod
and captured bass on a hand-tied hook.
The darkness is selective.
It closes only certain doors,

particular hallways—the closest ones.

This worries people: they blame him.
I blame him. No one likes to be forgotten.
He keeps lists to stop forgetting—
short stacks of paper next to each phone:
dinner Thursday, bring light bulbs next door,
Saturday birthday, Kate said okay,
grandkids prefer juice.
The calendar looms, presents daily possibilities
of things to be lost.

By summoning them,
repeatedly and with everyone he knows,
he lights a fire against the woods outside,
the narrowing shadows.
He polishes what's left.

Proof

Rose Heely with her blue hair proved to my father
in the fifth grade that it mattered how one spoke
if you wanted anyone else to listen.

Boys and girls, if I tell you that building is burning,
but my voice is flat and dull,
(here she grew tired and limp-shouldered),
if I mumble and monotone my way
through the warning, you'd all likely burn to death.

Students scooted in hard chairs,
checked their limbs weren't swallowed
in flame. Then Rose Heely shrieked,
one hand glued to her forehead, two long reaper
fingers pointing a curse out the other window,
her voice a danger bell that struck
their stomachs and feet soles. *FIRE FIRE FIRE!*
Rose roared,
her body a jumping bean, tossed jacks
sprouting and hopping in ways the children,
if asked to calculate the possibilities,
would never have guessed.

Her glasses bounced. Her voice hit
every key on a xylophone of panic and flight.
For all that is good and holy, children,
SAVE yourselves!

Some swooned. Boys wept for their mothers.
A girl in a blue smock ran
to the wall's extinguisher. Others sat, motionless
potato sacks in anticipation of singed flesh
until…Rose Heely grew still. *And that,*
dear boys and girls, is your lesson in inflection.

Air left the room with children's
exhalations, their sure feeling of cool skin

under fingertips. I'm there in the small galaxy
of my father's iris, a waiting
bloom, undeniable hurtling thing
that will knock the wind out of him.
I'm defying science, trying across the realms
of space-time to get him to look back
out that window,
heed Rose's warning.

Fire, Daddy, fire.
It's coming to burn you,
sure as spirits.
You can stop it. You can save me
from what you're going to do.
Can't you hear that in my voice?

Custom Games

A group of entrepreneurs at the next table
brainstorms. They're thinking outside the box,
providing deliverables,
saying things like "custom-made"
and "take the lead on that one, Jeff."
Is it cotton, 100% cotton?
Jeff asks the woman next to him.
That's the game, he says, *100%*
of anything is special.

So much business speak, I want
to throw hot coffee,
lift Jeff by his power tie,
tell him people aren't that stupid.

They call these moments
"grief events." Small heart breaks.
Never losing your loved one all at once.
Just a steady progression of pie charts
plotting before and after.

My father played these games
in suit and wingtip
for forty years, drove Boston to Bangor,
winning it all. What percentage
of his memories remain?
What's special enough to keep
away from this monster rioting
through his frontal lobe, stealing
file folders marked
yesterday, July, grandchildren?

Our primitive brains
like puzzles and old photographs.
Play games, his neurologists answer.
Meet him where he is right now.
What games does your father like to play?

A photo. July 1980.
Dad stands handsome,
laughing and muscled in Lake Sugden.
I'm midair, tossed high above the water,
bird taking wing
in a Kermit the Frog swimsuit.
The game is one he invented:
I spin four cardinal directions,
he catches me 100% of the time.

The trick was landing
true north. You can tell
from his rugged denim cutoffs
and fisherman's cap,
from the way he's thrown me
and stands like a compass,
that he is a man
who has everything he needs.

Today, at the Doctor's Office

Dad says *stop.*
Meaning, look at the photograph
on the wall, fall foliage
orange and red, dusty
shades of brown, reminding him
of the New England hillside.
He points to a path out,
says *Paul and I used to walk right there,*
right there along that trail.

Which memory does this scene
resurrect? One he will talk about
for days: burning leaves, stocked
ponds, birds rising into Cape Cod
dusks where dogs howled and shells
riddled the ground.

The doctors call his obsessions
perseveration—a symptom
of memories that leave him,
ones he'd rather cage
and release on his own.
They repeat on a loop
until he is finished.

I touch the frame.
Well, there were more bushes,
juniper berries and something else…
I can't recall.
Rustled hundreds of grouse
with a single shot…

How will he feel
when,
by the time we reach the car,
this picture has risen
and flown away

as easily as my mother's tiny wrist?

I take his hand, remember
how he smelled
of the woods when he came home
from hunting, and I was young.

An Increased Risk of Wandering

The parties in the hallway
had to stop.
Three a.m. and they're carrying on,
clinking glasses,
hooting and laughing like animals.
He must imagine Greek waiters
hauling trays of ice water and martinis
that never spill, stuffed olives the center
of some cosmic party gyroscope,
each drink's surface a gimbal he wants
to spin but cannot, is not allowed
to consume anymore.
You're dead a long time, Kate,
so why not a drink?
My dad told me once he'd wrap
his car around a tree,
put a bullet in his head if I ever
put him in a home.
He left it the first day, ducked down
a staff hallway, hit a sprint
before the pastor and male nurse
shouted for but couldn't reach him,
running leeway into the pines.
We found him drinking
Famous Grouse at the Mexican place
two miles down Cedarcrest.
Walking back from a gun shop another day
with a heavy coat and bulging pockets.
Announced his intent to marry that woman.
Disown me. Move to Costa Rica
to catch sailfin, black marlin, dorados.
The hallway parties started then, an ear
hallucinating, nerves soaked, sundowning.
He's waiting for the day when
it is my mother's voice
he hears in that hallway at three a.m.,
saying *Fez, come out, have a drink.*

They get on that sailboat
he keeps trying to buy
from the *Marietta Daily Journal* ads,
his brain healed, her heart good.
My mom is twenty-two again,
bathed in white linen,
steadying the boat, priming the keel.

Bird

vi.

The radical otherness of birds is integral to their beauty and their value. They are always among us but never of us. They're the other world-dominating animals that evolution has produced, and their indifference to us ought to serve as a chastening reminder that we're not the measure of all things. The stories we tell about the past and imagine for the future are mental constructions that birds can do without... In every corner of the globe, in nests as small as walnuts or large as haystacks, chicks are pecking through their shells and into the light.

~from Jonathan Franzen, "Why Birds Matter"

Simulacrum

She's got a house on wheels, this other me,
one that goes anywhere.
It's small, all hard edges and simple.
One place to sleep, another to eat,
one to undress herself and others,
a radio playing low blues
over the porch wherever she stops.
Spells ago, she stopped worrying
about a man or mortgage or dinner.

She haunts late dark smoky places.
Men feel the light brush
of wings each time she dances alone,
white tequila cool as any sunrise
in her hands. Criminal.

It's a ghost, what they feel,
turning away from her heat
when *Born on the Bayou*
churns on the jukebox,
her jeans and that tattoo whirling,
silver stud in her nose
catching all the light in the room.

And if you followed her home,
she'd show you empty cabinets
where nothing is kept
except feathers
floating through tiny kitchen windows.
A slain angel falling,
over and again, into the clean path
of a new life.

Like hair that can't be swept back
falling over her shoulder
or that picture of dandelion seeds,
useless as parasols
against slanted rain.

Birds of North America

Against the neighbor's house,
across a slash of pine and oak,
a flash of red.

Flight realized in cardinal,
bone, and feather.

Its crimson body streaks
a path, arcs tipsily through sunlight.

Luck wrought
by a cross-section of sun:

only ten minutes later,
the cardinal would have been lost in shadow.

Like purple martins and bluebirds
that pass in darkness,

one vermilion wing leaves me
coveting song.

Practice

What is it about the way we open a window
that does more than open a window?

At night, I usher in the darkness,
close the blinds,

shut the eyes of our home
to light's thickening absence,

uncertain what danger it is I think
I'm sealing in or out.

In morning, before the others wake,
I retrace those evening steps,

re-open what I'd closed before,
lifting the string of each veil,

let in what's been waiting in the dark:
cricket, owl, clawed bears, lightning storms.

I vow to woo the bright wild day and wed
those murky shadows that swim and lurk.

Groundwater Spell

i.

I'm haunted by shotgun shacks
and ramshackle gardens.
There are no natural lakes in Georgia,
only the ones created by engineers,
their controlled deluge and dammed rivers.

ii.

Imagine Acworth's buried post offices,
barns and vegetable stands
in a soup of the Chattahoochee,
the Etowah, the Coosawattee—
rivers I have floated down with my children.
Whose life did we pass over in our red speedboat
on joyriding July days?

iii.

How many preachers left their churchyards,
children rolled out of beds forever unmade?
Are there carpenters' makeshift tools,
cooks' rusty spoons? What of wedding dresses
worn by women left at the altar of rising water?
Or candlesticks war widows snubbed
before cold suppers?

iv.

Why not pulverized bones?
A farmer or professor who refused
to leave his land despite town postings,
deaf hermit whose cabin knew no map.
Before the reservoir broke, jealous mistress
who bound herself to a porch by leather belt.

v.

Not knowing what's baptized with longleaf pine
when one draws a circle on a map
and says *Everything goes,*
we speed on. We leave gasoline spirals,
our wake a flying maple seed unfolding.

vi.

To tell what's down there
in watery dark,
we need a diver:

one who'd surface and speak
in tongues about weeds
and underwater snakes,
lost propellers and sunken canoes.

Maybe a hand like petrified wood
would reach out in darkness
like Christ of the Abyss,
shrouded in trench moss and catfish.

vii.

One skeletal road
littered with broken pews
might be visible
past the silenced town bell
where sunflower fields grew,

their fiery crowns like faces
staring at a now-submerged wishing well,
its mouth a gate where water
enters a state beyond
the ones we know.

viii.

Past aquifers and wild bedrock,
how can we be sure
what will become relic,
waterlogged artifact,
archaeology of the muck?

What silt and pollen like snow
will ripple down?

So we drop lines into that flooded deep,
the dark shimmering past and valleys.
We fit our lures with fat worms
and shining scales,
teasing what lives there
to bite.

A Terrible Fish Comes to Me in Dreams

Some say it's a sign of fortune.
But when I wake,
I can't recall what kind of fish
hovered beneath the lake's horizon
in those ill-fated chases.
No net or barb or hook,
no bobber or line or worm
could capture the dark body
that shows up under houses,
off docks, under secret doors
and entryways to dreamscapes
and rivers and ancient secrets.
Big as a human,
it is a beast I cannot catch,
shadowy form that scuttles,
never surfacing.
Prehistoric, elusive, spotted.
Carp-like catfish, sturgeon,
or coelacanth, primordial
and primitive koi or silver tarpon,
its bottom-feeding barbels
dare me to jump in those waters
or else: grow gills,
breathe water and return
to the depths
from which I came.

She Divides Her Time

So what if I want all the places:
Columbian mountains, iguanas
and pebbled beaches in Costa Rica,
pura vida and sea alligators and four o'clock rain?

I want the sun and how it sets
in Western North Carolina, fog
and sweetgum trees and open doors.
Swift road slope winding down
to the Pacific at Manhattan Beach.
Indian trains. Chinese rivers. Irish lakes.

Amelia Island with its abandoned forts
and rising submarines.
Hemingway's six-toed cats off Duval Street,
the Gulf's swift tides,
dark evenings in Finland and cold vodka.
A spider lobster, bigger than my children, in Japan.
Michocoa's butterflies
and a screen door on a Tahitian hut.
Tidal flats in Louisiana.
Unspeakable black lava in Hawaii.
I want the glaciers, all of them.

Let them break my body
and be one
giant map of expanding light,
one star exploding, sinking
into a red hot core,
not dividing, but multiplying.

Give me the Marianas Trench
my fish-heart desires.
Because diving to the bottom
means I don't have to divide anything,
not my time or yours, not culture or tongues
or this hungry baby that the world keeps
feeding its foolish *rest easy*.

Washing

Let me be the white shirt
hung to dry
on the clothesline—
filled with wind,

blooming and animated
in its dance
as though there were
a body inside,

as if the pins
clipped to each shoulder
holding fabric to the greater
scaffold of weathered rope
prevented flight—

shirt climbing the skies,
cotton bird
charged with light,
almost clear.

Something Wicked Comes to the Carolina Coast

It wouldn't have been a terrible way to die
after so much sunshine, days romping in the sand,

hours leading my children through lukewarm tide pools,
chasing crabs, dragging buckets back to the beach house

before dinner and showers. If it all ended
with that Atlantic storm, if something wicked

and beautiful hid in the covers of dark clouds
like stirring bodies under the heat of summer sheets

and came for us in the Carolina sand,
who would stop its blinding fury?

I thought of my daughter, so otherworldly,
folding her body into origami as she stacked beach stones.

My son on a surfboard, triumphant in his newly-formed
muscles, angling his body though the surf.

My husband, knee-deep in the whitecaps, casting his line
near baby sharks, their mothers long gone on patrol.

And what will he reel in from those depths?
Maybe the Milky Way, that wild orange of star or planet,

or my friends, their raucous card games and curses
echoing down the long table after the children are asleep

before we retire to the private tides
of our own beds.

When I opened the porch door to half-light, plum dusk
and saw the paw of a giant cloud plodding

across the sky fast as a scythe, I thought, *well,*

we may never leave this house

by the sea. The world may end tonight, and here.
Unless it was me emerging from the deep at hook's end:

a naked and bioluminescent creature, refusing to go.

Wake Up Call

A rooster crows on the far side of sunrise,
an improbable call. No homestead here. No hens.

You're sure there shouldn't be roosters in suburbia,
but his muted alarm returns, fairly distant:

the moon is gone. Get going, you. So you do,
in your ashen robe with your pale coffee.

You imagine his cocky strut on cracked corn, hackle
and saddle feathers ruffling: *get going.* You do.

He cockadoodles in dimness, croons a territorial brag
too late for any farm. He does not belong,

but you do? Behind some garden fence, he's all proud swagger,
brazen comb, red wattle blazing like fire in stacked straw.

He stifles the cul-de-sac's sallow yawn. You comb your hair,
ruffle your shirt: *get going.* And you, strange bird, you do.

ACKNOWLEDGMENTS

Further thanks to the journals in which these poems have appeared in current or earlier forms:

The Blue Mountain Review
Five Points
Forum: Phi Kappa Phi
Halcyone
High Shelf Press
Josephine Quarterly
Pangyrus
River Heron Review
Sanctuary
Sea Stories
Slant
Water~Stone
Wicked Alice

Some of these poems may have appeared in the chapbook *If Not an Apple* (La Vita Poetica), 2006.

Psalm 36:5-9. Thank you to The Hambidge Center for its generous Artist Residency, Ignatius House for quiet retreats ("There is no way of telling people that they are all walking around shining like the sun," says Thomas Merton), and to the Glen East Workshop at Mount Holyoke College. Thank you to the Georgia Writer's Association, Callanwolde Fine Arts Center, and Cobb County Public Library's Poets Read program.

Thank you to the following poets, writers, and mentors whose tutelage touched this collection in ways both big and small during the past fifteen years: Cecilia Woloch, Laura Newbern, Ralph Tejeda Wilson, William Walsh, William Wright, Cheryl Stiles, Kathy Kincer, Donna Coffee Little, Adrian Blevins, Leon Stokesbury, Beth Gylys, and Kate McConnaughey. Thank you to my fellow poets and classmates at UGA, Agnes Scott, GSU, KSU, and Reinhardt University. And for Kathy May, where you go I will go.

Fesuk, a Massachusetts native, teaches English in Marietta, Georgia and has earned degrees from the University of Georgia, Agnes Scott College, Kennesaw State University, and, most recently, the Etowah Valley MFA from Reinhardt University. *Mamabird* is her first full-length book. Fesuk studied English and Creative Writing in the doctoral program at Georgia State University and was a Georgia Author of the Year Award nominee for her chapbook *If Not an Apple* (La Vita Poetica Press). She worked as Poet in Residence at The Walker School, served as Creative Writer in Residence at the Kennesaw Mountain Writing Project, and published poems that can be found in more than forty journals including *Five Points, Poet Lore, The Pedestal, Slant, Atlanta Review*, and *Wicked Alice*. "To Other Parents in June," from which this collection derives its name, is nominated for a 2020 Pushcart Prize.

www.ingramcontent.com/pod-product-compliance
Lightning Source LLC
Chambersburg PA
CBHW021153090426
42740CB00008B/1071